D1601114

Breakfast with
Allen Ginsberg

Esther Cohen

Pleasure Boat Studio: A Literary Press
New York

Breakfast with Allen Ginsberg

By Esther Cohen

ISBN 978-1-7364799-3-3

Library of Congress Control Number: 2016948738

Design and Cover by Laura Tolkow

Pleasure Boat Studio books are available through:

Bookshop

Baker & Taylor

Ingram

Amazon.com

Barnes and Noble

Pleasureboatstudio.com

for

Ahava Esther Dolpha-Odabashian

I hope she likes a poem or two

.

An imprecise while ago, I started writing a
poem a day. As an exercise. On the Internet,
on a site with the unfortunate name of
BLOG. The poems are a short, funny record
(not a Memoir. Not laden with Significance,
either) of what happens to me each day.
Most of the time, it's very little.

overheardec.substack.com
esthercohen.com

Esther Cohen
https://overheardec.substack.com
917 710-5633

1 Allen Ginsberg
or I Wanted to Be a Poet

Part One

When I moved to New York City
in the '70s from Ansonia small
factory town in Connecticut
Allen G was who I wanted to meet
Jean Boudin
Good Beat Poet
said Allen will see anyone
if they'll buy him breakfast
Found his number from Kenneth Koch
and I office temp at Rochester Button
had plenty of breakfast money
In the diner he was Allen Ginsberg
I was Esther Cohen
Ask me anything he said in exchange
for two eggs
Can I be
a poet like you

Not having read even one word
he said You Are a Poet
Esther Cohen
Can I quote you I asked
You have my lifetime permission
he said and all these years later I am

Part Two

A few weeks ago at a poet's retreat
in San Miguel de Allende British
poet laureate a Sir did not like
my poems You he said infusing You
with Ultimate British Disdain You
he repeated are in the same category
as that American poet
Allen Ginsberg
At long last I replied
At long last

2 How to Write a Poem

Lesson 1

Start here
or over there
First words matter
Start is better
than *begin* Where
you go up to you
Try to go
where you can find
your best poem

Lesson 2

You want
to write
OK Just
sit right there

Don't move
Then write
words down

Lesson 3

Some days
no poems
Wait

3 Pennysaver

Do you want
help from me
Here's what I
can do if you ask if you call
don't send me an email
I don't like emails
I can ORGANIZE
I can clean
I actually like CLEANING
I had a client who
used the word DAZZLE
in relation to me
I can cook although honestly
I am a so-so cook
OK with easy chicken
I can babysit if the baby's
just eating and sleeping
I actually like
even love

laundry
I could do laundry
all day long
Do you have
a lot of laundry?
I can clean out
attics pantries basements
not a sentimental person
your grandmother's papers
can go if I'm in charge
if you do hire me
how's one day a week
my guess is you
will be pleasantly
surprised

4 Last Night As Always

I called Bruce
although he is the best
telephone person
he nearly always says
Can I Call You Back?
He is Doing Something Else
Last night he was
cutting up zucchini
I asked him why
he can't talk to me
the same time
he cuts his zucchini
but he can't
Later he calls back to explain
What Happened the Last Few Days
Mike the painter
has landlord problems
red flying squirrel still eating
Bruce's grapes

He hired Harry
psychic animal catcher
to catch the flying squirrel
I listen thinking words
are the musical notes I love

5 What we say

My friend Lisa
wonderful painter
paintings at
West Kortright Center
her friends were there
first woman I met
light linen dress
perfect color
beads that might
have been ivory
she's a painter too
sitting on an outside bench
facing Delaware county green
I am a Midwesterner
she said
I like Jews
married two
Sam Katz
then number two

we met at an
East Village
Vegan restaurant
six kids
paintings
on the street
he lost both legs
in an accident
funny thing
he became
a happier person
can you
believe that she said
96 now
What else
would you
like to know?

6 What We Remember

Michael Kreiger's cousin name
   it might be Henry
I don't quite remember I do know he
kissed me in seventh grade standing
   by a big oak tree he
put his hand on my back
   right on my bra strap my bra
looked like two peanut shells
   connected with nylon string
my first memorable kiss his hand
was there on my back forever lived
   in another town so
he wrote me a letter I don't remember
   his words but he
drew a picture of the outline of his hand
and I could feel it there

7 Aryeh

Don't go down the Israeli aisle advised
Ulla longtime book professional
first time I went
to the Frankfurt Book Fair
years ago if she had warned me
about the Chinese aisle my life
might have been different
Israeli aisle I entered first
two men one round close to the ground
other long thin together
a good set of salt shakers
Three of us after that They taught
philosophy wanted to start
publishing company In the eighties
We did
And then what
What is this story's arc
I can only tell you today
The rest a novel

Today I am teaching a class
in a shelter where the short round one
he became my close friend family
member we said we were true relatives
he lived in the shelter sixteen years
Today the woman who runs the building
she liked him today she said
because he is back
    in Jerusalem because his life has taken
its hundredth turn today someone
he doesn't know will clear out his room
Goethe Beckett Musil Kafka
    valuable volumes of Proust
come to the lobby she said
take books home
you'll remember him more

8 Labels

Even hard for me
to throw away one shoe
silver Clergerie sandal
no longer available
one under my bed
in case the other one
(where did it go) reappears
this morning
three years of waiting
for the right shoe
I brought my silver sandal
to our basement
made a sign for the empty recycling bin
SHOES

_9_ We Celebrate

everything every single holiday
inviting people over
to eat
people my flowers my trees
we cook they cook
we all drink Peter often
makes holiday drinks
mango tequila surprise
Bruce sautés his greens
uses his own garlic
we all sit together somewhere
Memorial Day the Fourth of July
when what we want
what we always want
to invite people over to eat

10 Or Else

I am up
don't want to do
all that is on
the big list
exercise for instance
Woman I don't like much
declared
we she meant me
have to exercise
four times a week
Or Else

11 Grandparenting

Saturday night we invited neighbors
for champagne young blond they
have two boys sixteen months apart
in October they'll
have a third boy
we like them elevator
friends I wanted them to tell us
what their parents did right and wrong
nervous about the Grandparent Thing
having a child being a parent
one of those subjects too many
Hallmarky adjectives
few people tell the truth
polite blond neighbors spoke a long list:
unfortunate intrusiveness
their words now in a new notebook
called Bad Grandparenting

Annie said her daughter-in-law said
you had your child this one is mine
daughter-in-law is right
even so

12 Rose

Rose sits on the right hand side
of the flea market every single Sunday
resplendent in purple fur hat
long red coat
smile wide as a schoolyard
we are addicted to Rose's clothing pile
six dollars for clothing
someone else bought once
wore to a prom a first date
someone else
thought a dark green velvet dress suitable
for all occasions Me too and
on a good week I go to Rose
excavate extract
golden boots ten dollars yesterday
talk to Rose for her continual advice
You need a new raincoat Esther
everyone does and she points
to the pile to a turquoise rain poncho

perfect one day Little Richard came
Twice a year he visited her warehouse
in the Bronx he fills up a small
yellow bus wow I said
when Rose told me that
Did you really believe
you were my only customer
Rose replied

13 This Time of Year

This time of year every year around this
same week because there is a new year
which is one of those reality illusion
things is January first any different from
December first how is forty-nine different
from fifty numbers are only absolute if you
believe they are, and I don't, I say to Peter
I'd like to talk to you about my writing he
laughs and says I've heard that before what
do you want to say? He is never impatient
with me. I'm the one who is impatient. I
want to tell him I am older and I'm afraid
that I will never write a good sentence
and what if I don't. I had a psychiatrist
once whom I told that to. What if all my
sentences were bad? It took me months to
tell her. "Go home," she said. "Write as
many bad sentences as you can." I wrote

bad sentences for about a year. The chicken
clucked. Still one of my favorite sentences.
A clucking chicken named Ralph. Every
year, I worry about writing the wrong
sentence, even though I have hundreds
of notebooks good pen the opportunity I
don't know that it will be the right year
will it be now and the place where the good
sentence will emerge probably it will appear
on our porch while I am sitting on the
purple divan no springs no springs doesn't
matter I might be facing east holding my
favorite gray notebook micro pen I've tried
many I will sit trying hard not to think of
good sentences or bad ones but because it
will be let's say February early morning
and because of what happened two days
before not in the world but in my ordinary
life and because of an email or a phone
call or Obama or the color of roses on
the table bright deep red then when the
circumstances line up the way moons do
then I will finally after so many years write
my secret sentence

14 Nuts.com

This morning I called
Nuts.com
man named Frank
told me that there
was No Good Reason
why my nuts which
their system shows
were delivered January
8 are Still Not Here
Maybe said Frank
they are
on the truck
or maybe just
an example
of something being
Real Life Nuts

15 Bentley the Dog

young family came to ski
we rent our house
lost their home
in Hurricane Sandy
shell shocked still
old dog Bentley
with them
gone
when they
came home from skiing
blind and deaf
small pug
serious arthritis
they screamed
shouted
called police
walked in circles
in our field
no one slept

wolves coyotes

what happens in country dark

at dawn

father began to search

there was Bentley

happy

on a nearby hill

16 How To Cure Hashimoto's Disease

I left One Medical
technology medical practice
my body
an Apple device
doctors stood
at the Genius Bar
now while I am
in between
official information
I google Hashimoto's
to see what I can do
read Coping essays
including one
from a woman
who wrote
an unreadable
book free excerpts
on line
she said

STRESS HAS TO BE
ENTIRELY ELIMINATED
does she mean
Other People
News
The Big World
Crazy Republicans
maybe I'll email
her today
and ask her to explain
If she does
I'll let you know

17 How's the Weather

There was a time
I wrote about
my grandmother
left Bacau Romania
for Grand Forks North Dakota
husband four kids
farmers everywhere
she felt lost
moved to New Haven
where I was born
one day Uncle Alex
in L.A. drove up
in a gold Cadillac
could have
been a Buick the family
said Cadillac ran upstairs
to our apartment
I was 5 years old
Come On Ma You're Moving

to California
in what seemed
like an hour maybe it was
she got into
my Uncle Alex's car
drove off to a place
where she was finally
happy wrote me
a lifetime of letters
each one beginning
the same way
This Weather is Perfect
what she always said

18 Wanda

Wanda was here
when I moved in
she was an Old Lady
maybe younger
than I am NOW
thin
her middle name
puff of never moving white hair
high high heels
worked on 34th Street
in an office
went shopping
every single Saturday
for clothes she called Outfits
hair and nails done
once a week
at least
Sunday
she did laundry

got even thinner
heels remained high
we would talk
in the laundry room
Wanda
would mention weather
usually Not Good
She didn't like
summer or winter either
lived in a studio
no visitors
super never
went inside
one day
a month ago
Wanda asked me
to help her into
a car service
to go to
her hairdresser
a week later
she fell in her room
died a few
days later

super came
to tell me
yesterday
Wanda
didn't have
a telephone
land line or cell
she left six
million dollars
no one knows
where the money
came from or
where it will
all go now

19 Otto or Einstein's friend

I can't imagine
actually writing a poem
about how Einstein was right
More Up My Alley is this
Einstein had a
partner
named OTTO Appealing
scientist tiny
Princeton
political man
We had dinner with him
a few times
because Bess
kind of a relative
though not entirely
large large woman
she owned one style
of dress
navy and black

two each she was
married to Harry
crazy about Otto
and he her they
loved each other
big and small
came to my apartment
for dinner
we were their excuse
if they were with us
just like teenagers
All Was Well
Otto told
Einstein stories
I thought I'd
remember forever but
All I remember is
Otto and Bess

20 Ten Ways To Be a Writer

1. Sit somewhere. It's hard to write if you're standing up. Though you can do it if you have no choice.

2. Time of day doesn't matter. It could be dawn or 4 PM or after you've binge-watched many episodes of *The Good Wife*.

3. Figure out what you're going to write WITH. I like pens with names like Ultra Fine. My friend Bruce likes THICK. Many people write on laptops.

4. If it's a pen you choose, you need paper. Paper is as tricky as pens. Lines or not. Notebooks and what size they will be.

5. Have something to drink nearby. Coffee, tea, water, juice. A glass of white wine, expensive or cheap. Red, too, is satisfactory. Be prepared for thirst.

6. Reading matter. You need a good book in the vicinity. For inspiration. A book by

your favorite author, or one of them. Grace
Paley is always there for me.

7. Don't worry. There are many things
you might worry about before you write.
Do I Have Anything To Say always a Big
Worry. Eliminate that sentence from your
concerns for now. There's plenty of time to
consider that question later.

8. Forget about emails, at least for a little
while. Also, laundry.

9. Banish thoughts that you will never be
Nabokov or Toni Morrison.

10. You are ready. Put your pen into
your hand (or, your hand onto the keys) and
begin with the word NOW. And see what
happens next.

21 Tell Me if You Can

some of us
tell each other
as much as we can
we are together
in this life
what happened
how I feel
we listen
we talk
by the words
we say
by the words
we never say
some of us
never let
other people
finish their stories
sentences even
impatient

we don't wait
to hear an ending
or two
some of us
will never say
anything at all
so others of us
will have to
imagine those stories
for ourselves

22 Somewhere Else

We are on our way
somewhere else
what we
decide
to see
how we do that
what life
looks like
what other people's
lives look like
many of us
seek out what
we know
The unfamiliar
blue
you've never
seen before
a face
a phrase

what we don't know
is what
can change
us all

23 Vietnam

Today I want
to tell you
a story said
our intrepid guide
How my sister
got engaged to
a man who
fixed engines Right
before their wedding
he disappeared
We heard that
boat people
took him
Ten years
went by One
night he
knocked at
our door We
thought he

was a ghost
Now they live
in Pittsburgh
She runs
a nail parlor
He has
a good job
If you saw them
you wouldn't
know any
of this

24 Veng Tells a True Story

We kept our money
in gold Veng said When
the Khmer Rouge came
my father hid our gold
in a well with dirty water
where no one would drink
He and my mother went
to the well after the war
All our money was gone
My mother cried
One day when my father
was walking he saw
three men drinking liquor
One of the men said
'you look so unhappy I will
buy you a drink and you
will feel better OK
said my father
The man was

a fortune teller My father
didn't believe in them
Still he told the stranger
his problem You're
in luck he told my father
Your money is still
in the well The next day
he went to the well
with my uncle and his
money was right there
He and the strange man
became like brothers
This is Cambodia
said Veng

25 Tourists, or Other People

How would I feel
when 18 small brown tourists
from Vietnam
came to see
how big white people
lived entered
my rent-stabilized
apartment to watch me
eat a bagel schmeered
with cream cheese I would
offer them arbitrary
explanations
when they examined
my shoes particularly my
red suede sandals
pink laces if they
saw my Big TV
home to Bob's Burgers
looked inside my refrigerator

examining Paul Newman's
salad dressing big bottle
of Heinz ketchup
asked what I thought about war
or duty governments
and love I wonder
what I'd want to say

26 A New Poem

Yesterday someone I don't know
whose name sounds like Mia
but it isn't quite Mia she wrote to me
asked me the question
WHAT IS A POEM
How did she find me to ask
That is a poem
Dear Almost Mia
I can't tell you
what a poem is
although
there are
infinite definitions
I often buy
books where experts
explain
what poems are
They are very sure
Not me For me

a poem is a moon

or a whisper

Even an unforgettable

wail A poem

can even be a person

Yesterday I saw

an old old woman

sitting on a bench

on 68th Street

and Broadway

and she

was absolutely

a poem

27 DEAR ESTHER COHEN

OH DEAR NO
What you sent
me can't possibly
be POEMS
Something else
maybe but I
as EDITOR of
a JOURNAL
for many many
(there is actually a third
many) years
don't know
the word for
what you sent
And although I
tell everyone
to try us again
I'm not sure
about YOU

28 Turkish Food

Peter is Armenian
I believe in forgiveness
He does too
Not to go to a Turkish restaurant
seems silly
People who work there
nothing to do
with what happened
to his family Governments
and people
not the same
We both believe
holding on is never
a good idea
though this
is an even so poem
even so time
to go to dinner we don't
go often

to Turkish restaurants

though of course

we like them

29 Tell Me Anything

Some people
I am one of them
want to know everything
even when
it is absolutely
none of my business
want to know why
tea party woman across the street
we only said hello once or twice
she said a weather sentence
hot or *cold* more or less
I want to know why she
left her husband
I know absolutely nothing of him
just George his name
he did something with trucks

Some people why are we like this
I was born listening
to Julia C. Steele
next-door neighbor
small factory town
where I grew up
a librarian she was having
an affair with a married woman
a long time ago
they seemed happy
I didn't know what an affair was
thought it was a party
they seemed happy
married woman
a fifth-grade teacher
my father went to grammar school
with her when I told him
what was happening how did I even
know he said Don't Be Crazy
went back to reading
The New York Times
which he didn't believe
was crazy at all
a few years later

Julia C. Steele ran away
with the fifth-grade teacher
actually got into a red car
she drove away
didn't say goodbye
didn't come back my father
kind man serious man
I loved my father said
Why are they leaving

they love one another
I said How do you
know he asked
They look happy
I said
How does happy look
My father asked
He was a logical man
Like them
I told him
Just like them

30 Eva Balco

Round babysitter Eva Balco
infinite patience
all characters
in every play I wrote often
based on neighbors
tiny family husband named Jake
he was big we often
discussed Jake
one day I asked
what Jake was like
who was he when they met
when they married
who was Jake right now
Jake is Elvis Presley
said Eva Balco
she laughed
and I laughed too
One day she said
You'll know what

I mean And even though
I didn't understand
not really way before
my own Elvis Presleys
I had a classic
black-and-white
notebook
wrote it down
Eva Balco's husband Jake
is Elvis Presley
because I knew one day
very soon
I'd understand

31 Didier Bongo

Didier Bongo
Benin-born taxi driver
told me today
there are no Esther Cohens
not even one
in Benin
he is not
the only Didier Bongo
there
Maybe
he speculated
New York
is the only place
for us both

32 Ken

Ken lives across the street
Old-style pre-hip hop
You're in the Navy Now tattoo
chain smoker one cigarette
behind his right ear
at all times Ken
never liked him much
until this summer Hilda
gentle gardening wife
Hilda died last May
Ken drove a truck
for 41 years
a very big truck
he didn't like when people
asked if he was a trucker
he couldn't say why not
When Hilda died
he held her hand
something of Hilda

lives in Ken and when he
comes over
every single afternoon
at four says he's coming by
free coffee and cookies
though he didn't come
across the road for 14 years
he walks over as though
he always has
it's OK with me
because I see Hilda
inside Ken
when he tells us
over and over
again his one long
story about baking trucks
and Brooklyn I can see Hilda
and she's smiling

Two Beryl Goldbergs

Years ago Beryl Goldberg
got mail for another Beryl Goldberg
they'd make life easier
one apartment together
and when they did
to celebrate they held
a Beryl Goldberg party
I thought I should bring
another Esther Cohen
found one in the phone book
nearby therapist
my address is 66 West 77th
77 West 88th was hers
we were number mates
on the phone I talked her
into coming to
Beryl Goldberg's party
She asked

if other Esther Cohens

would appear

we never saw each other again

34 Ahava

One week ago today
only one week ago
today seems like
a long year
after the baby
was born when we
got into a cab to
take a shower cab driver
asked why we were at
Roosevelt Hospital he
was the first person
we told about the baby's birth
Let me give you some advice
he said Maybe it's more
just information
My granddaughter is 5 months old
Do you want to know the difference
between our generation
and theirs? Our daughter's first

meal was at Taco Bell
Her daughter was fed an
organic avocado And here's
another tip Don't say
anything but *yes*

35 Having a Baby

I was at a meeting
about God Knows What
Peter working on
a trailer for his movie
Noah called to say
Chesray's labor
had begun
she would come
to our apartment
with her doula
we were waiting waiting for life
to begin real person
arms legs
eyes and a heart
fluorescent lights
all exhausted
nervous then in awe
Could This Be What Life Is
could it be this simple

Ahava
born at 6:45 AM
she who brings love to this world
eight pound baby
we all stood there
knowing what happened
as common as air
as common as breath
as common
as life

36 Always

Birth
of a child
birth of thousands
of children
what she
needs to live
what do they need
besides love
and food
work one day
some good friends
We often
run in small circles
Friend so
scheduled
he doesn't have time
to watch French murder
mystery dreams of the day
when he can sit and sit

drinking lattes
We try making
sense of what
does not lend
itself to logic
maybe if you
are a mathematician
scientist
person
who believes
in the ability to understand
what birth means
how it feels
to watch
a baby sleep
maybe if you are someone
who thinks life
has answers
Here I am sitting near
a tree so beautiful
it is more than a tree
here I am
trying to tell you
what it means

that a baby
is nearby
always
a tree
a baby nearby

37 True

I am George Koffi
I have 5.5 million USD (DOLLARS!)
to put into your account
Please send me Some Information
and I'll Begin The Process
Do Not Be Angry With Me
I request this information
I do not want to fall VICTIM
and you are my
Only Hope and I
Am Yours

38 Bruce Again

When the kids
arrived last night
night before
Thanksgiving
they asked Bruce
who is coming
this year he
took out
his yellow pad
long list written
with a Sharpie
Here's who's
not coming
he said
and then
he read his list

39 Delores

My daughter Josephine
some family I have
a reality show
I love every single one
my daughter Josephine
do you remember I have
six children
the baby is 52 that doesn't qualify
for baby unless
you're her mother
my daughter Josephine
she is sixty this year
a wild card she's the smartest
one had a baby at 17
first grandchild she married Tom
handsome guy panhandling
on the street in Catskill New York
I saw him the first time
and I said to myself

Josephine's going
to marry Tom
Everyone's
got to have
a first husband

40 Bernie

My friend
Laura's father Bernie
(he introduced us)
one of my all-time
favorite voices
I would like to go to Queens
record Bernie shouting
ESTA explaining
what he thinks
of Al Sharpton
(likes him) labor movement
(oy vey)
Rachel Maddow (good)
Orthodox neighbors
in Queens
(generous people
the man tied his shoes)
what's wrong with his
big toe (you don't

want to know)
how the nurse
changed his toe's dressing
(not good)
telephone systems
(he sells them)
why I am not rich
(no head for money
unfortunate)
He came into my office
by mistake fifteen
years ago got off
the elevator
on the wrong
floor walked right into
my room and shouted
what the hell
are you doing
in here

41 On our Way

We are on our way
somewhere else
what we
decide
to see
how we do that
what life
looks like
what other people's
lives look like
many of us
seek out what
we know
unfamiliar
blue
you've never
seen before
faces
a phrase

what we don't know
is what
can change
us all

42 Sleep With Me

Last night I listened
To *Sleep With Me*
ongoing podcast series
wildly boring narratives
told in a foolproof voice
rambling incoherent stories
work well for sleep
Years ago
four of us were
in a house in Greece
no electricity
We couldn't see
to read
at night so Cliff
told us details
of a trip and fall case he
worked on
He never got
to the case's

resolution
and every night
of our vacation
we slept

43 Attributes

Many years ago friend
sent me to a woman
who called
her job Head Hunter
her name
was Joyce Payton
(in case you
are worried her name
wasn't really Joyce Payton)
even though I didn't want
what everyone else called
A Real Job
I wanted a Fake Job
whatever that might be
Joyce Payton explained she
had a Very Important Exercise
to qualify for a Real Job
The exercise consisted
of writing my ATTRIBUTES

on a yellow pad clearly
so Joyce could read them
out loud to me
I wrote a very long list
of what I
considered My Strong Points
there are always
pistachio nuts
in my home
was one
Another
I know how
to make Lebanese style
Baba ganoush
Joyce did not
want to read my list
out loud but I told her
that was our tacit
agreement and so she
did although she made
it very clear my skills
had little to do with
Getting a Job
I made a

XEROX of the list
brought it home
to Harry who did an
impressive oral reading
he guaranteed that he
would hire me immediately
if he ever got a job

For years now
I've proposed an article
Eight Agents
One Husband
my title for years now
Illustrious Prestigious
Places that talk about
Writing have written
to me Though This Might
Be Funny (one woman
wrote that it could even
be Very Funny)
Such an Article
she really did say
Such an Article)
Dangerous
for Those of Us
in the business
Dangerous because

what if I named names?
I wrote her back
that if I'd had
eight husbands
I would want to
Tell The Reader
what their names
were but I am
perfectly willing
to make names up
NO NO NO she wrote
some things
are just taboo
few days ago
I had lunch with
Ilana young writer
we talked about
what we each
wanted to write
Eight agents one husband
I said
She just laughed

45 What Nora Roberts Said

Nora Roberts
she writes
ten times
more
than the rest
of us
here's what she
said in *The New Yorker*
just put
your ass
in the chair

46 Never

I keep thinking I should
write a Resolution poem
what I'd like to do
but never will
Tango Lessons
Portuguese
My friend Linda's advice
before she died
resolutions should
be mindless simple
Polish your nails red
I will never
learn Mandarin
do yoga every day
throw out thousands
of pieces of paper
I keep in a friendly
hopeful mound never accept
the word *never* in my head

I replace it with *maybe*
because it is
a better word

47 I Am the Embodiment of Infinite Possibilities (First Corinthian Baptist Church)

A few thousand people (yes)
wait in line for the third service
of the morning at the Black Church in
Harlem
my South African
daughter-in-law
Chesray Dolpha attends
most Sundays
I am not a stranger
to religious institutions
that aren't mine
As a child I often asked
friends to take me with them
this exploration
one of the ways
we can know each other
most of us want our selves

replicated
by our children
values mirrored reinforced
afraid of difference
we want proof that we
passed along
the right tradition
set of beliefs
right in how we lived
what we knew
stuck in our own dogma
I can sound
all-knowing absolute
but about almost everything
I'm unsure
our son fell in love
an African woman from Cape Town
I didn't know
what their life would be
different from mine
but how
at Chesray's church
we're embraced at the door
service loud and lively

People shout out
In front of us
tall black drag queen
in a sequined dress
waves her funeral home fan
three older women sit behind
from Milan people dance
we leave and go to brunch
I am entirely familiar
with brunch
together Chesray
and I two women
separated by what we know
what we learned as children
we order our coffees
Sunday eggs
knowing
difference and *hope*
are sisters

48 Dolly

We found out
yesterday
from a neighbor
that Dolly former
Waldorf Astoria manicurist
once she manicured
Fred Astaire's nails
Dolly told us all she
was a widow
but when she died
her tribute
at the nail parlor
around the corner
(she went twice a week
nail perfect
even her last week of life)
brother spoke
Dolly was not a widow
he said
ex-husband

owned the flower shop
right around the corner
and then on cue
her ex spoke up:
Here I Am

49 Pre-Used

And now at this point
insane moment
of age and longing
cusp and pinnacle
my arms are different arms
my dreams are always
interrupted
longing becomes more
I can no longer do
This or That
As much as I still want
Wake up wondering
How I no longer care
about why
when a day
is not just a day
but right now

50 Where My Family Came From

I don't know
No one said much
because they were
all anxious to be
Americans
Doctors etcetera
not Eastern European
peasants persecuted poor
Rivka my father's mother short and difficult
thin thin lips
widowed young she listened
to the radio all day long
English on the radio
my father bought her bread
he had to lie
about the price
everything
was too much
She might have had a sister

I think I met
her once her children
would be my relatives
I never saw them
My father's father
died before my life
I am *Esther* for his *Oscar*
is his life
part of mine?
I wonder now

Notes

My poems have appeared in many places. I
know that most people like to tell you which
poem was where. (*I'm Getting Older* was in
the *New York Times*. You probably want to
know that most of all. Some of my poems
have appeared in a few places. Some of
them are HERE for the first time.)

Wonderful photographer Matthew Septimus
and I have collaborated for years and years.
Many of these poems have his beautiful
accompanying photographs. You can see
them all on the NPR blog where we create
postcards for holidays: www.onbeing.org/
blog Matthew's other pictures are here.
www.matthewseptimus.com

So has Larry Bush and *Jewish Currents*, a
terrific magazine about secular Jews and
everything else. www.jewishcurrents.org.

My friend Meryl Meisler, photographer
extraordinaire, asked me for the Allen
Ginsberg poem. It's part of her amazing
book. www.merylmeisler.com.

Thank you to my first ever writing group,
which consists of the amazing Clarke sisters
Cheryl and Breena. We meet as often as
possible at Happy Hour in the Jade Hotel.

Other places my poems appeared:
*Alimentum, The Chronogram, Alte,
Brevitas, First Literary Review, One
Sentence Poems, Newsday, Na'amat Women,*
and *Women Around Town.*

My all time favorite graphic designer agreed
to make me a book, again. Thank you thank
you Laura Tolkow.

I wish every poet had a publisher like Jack
Estes and Pleasure Boat. Imagine being on
a pleasure boat with your poems.
www.pleasureboatstudio.com

And for Peter. Without Whom.